M1 Abrams

Written by David Doyle

In Action®

Cover Art by Don Greer

Line Illustrations by Todd Sturgell

Squadron Signal Publications

(Front Cover) A 3ACR Abrams blasts a stronghold in Tal'afar, opening the way for U.S. Special Forces and the First Battalion 26th Commandos Brigade (Kurdish Peshmerga militia) in September 2005.

(Back Cover) Heavy, but fast and powerful, an Abrams leans while cornering as it hurries to seal off Tal'afar, 70km northwest of al-Mawşil, in northern Iraq.

About the In Action® Series

In Action® books, despite the title of the genre, are books that trace the development of a single type of aircraft, armored vehicle, or ship from prototype to the final production variant. Experimental or "one-off" variants can also be included. Our first *In Action*® book was printed in 1971.

Hardcover ISBN 978-0-89747-733-8
Softcover ISBN 978-0-89747-734-5

Proudly printed in the U.S.A.
Copyright 2013 Squadron/Signal Publications
1115 Crowley Drive, Carrollton, TX 75006-1312 U.S.A.

Military/Combat Photographs and Snapshots

If you have any photos of aircraft, armor, soldiers, or ships of any nation, particularly wartime snapshots, why not share them with us and help make Squadron/Signal's books all the more interesting and complete in the future? Any photograph sent to us will be copied and returned. Electronic images are preferred. The donor will be fully credited for any photos used. Please send them to:

Squadron/Signal Publications
1115 Crowley Drive
Carrollton, TX 75006-1312 U.S.A.
www.SquadronSignalPublications.com

(Title Page) In an image fraught with the symbolism of the rapid and utter defeat of Saddam Hussein's regime during Operation Iraqi Freedom in 2003, two M1A1 Abrams main battle tanks (MBTs) from A Company, Task Force 1st Battalion, 35th Armor Regiment, 2nd Brigade Combat Team (BCT), 35th Armor Regiment, 1st Armored Division pause under the Hands of Victory monument in Ceremony Square, Baghdâd.

Acknowledgments

None of these books would be possible without a great deal of help from my friends, some old, some new. This is particularly true in the case of this book, where I leaned heavily on Tom Kailbourn; Donald P. Moriarty III, SFC (R); John Charvat, LTC(R); Michael Mummey, MSgt USMC(ret); Gary Owsley, USA(R); Scott Hamric, Third Armored Cavalry Regiment historian; and Russ Adams. My wonderful wife Denise as well deserves thanks, especially for willingly helping track down the photos for this book. All the photos presented in this book come from U.S. military sources unless otherwise noted.

Introduction

The Abrams was conceived during the height of the Cold War. Its designers and builders conceived a vehicle that would be fit to fight on a battlefield swarming with scores of Communist-manned tanks. Unable to match the theoretical enemy in numbers, engineers sought to create a vehicle that would technologically superior – with better armor protection, superior armament, and a far-advanced electronic suite that would enable its crew to "see" the battlefield, no matter what the conditions.

Also revolutionary was the tank's power plant. Previous U.S. tanks had been powered by reciprocating internal combustion engines – a variety of air- and liquid-cooled, naturally aspirated and turbo supercharged, carbureted and fuel-injected engines had been used heretofore. But the new tank had a new sort of powerplant: a Lycoming-designed (later also produced by Honeywell) 1,500-horsepower gas turbine.

This powerplant, while having a high fuel consumption, is lighter and smaller than Diesel engines of similar horsepower and it provides rapid acceleration. The engine also starts more easily in cold weather than does a Diesel, and provides instant power – without "warm up." The AGT-1500 design, while intended to burn JP-8 jet fuel, can also consume Diesel or gasoline.

Although the early versions of the Abrams relied on the same air conditioning system used by tankers for decades – opening the hatches and hoping for a breeze – the M1A2SEP features an Environmental Control Unit (ECU) in the bustle rack. While intended to cool the electronics inside the tank, the crew gets some associated benefits. Also in the crew comfort and sustainability arena – all versions of the Abrams include a ration heater which makes hot water with which MREs can be heated.

Fortunately, to date the Abrams has never had to fight the enemies that it was created to combat. Instead of facing dozens of tanks operating in lush forests and grasslands, the Abrams most often battles an enemy hidden beneath the sands of an arid desert – powerful land mines – with the somewhat understated moniker Improvised Explosive Devices (IEDs) are the biggest threat to Abrams's crews.

On those few occasions the Abrams has been engaged in tank-to-tank combat, the American main battle tank (MBT) has indeed targeted the vehicles it was designed to defeat – albeit its foes were not crewed by armies envisioned. In every instance the Abrams has handily and readily dispatched its opponents – well proving the soundness of the Abrams design in the role for which it was created.

Its new foes, however, have forced revisions and changes to the tanks' structure. With those improvements – often based on lessons learned in combat – in place, the Abrams offers its crew the maximum protection that can be provided on the battlefield.

These lessons have been learned – and the tuition paid in the blood of U.S. troops – in action in the Persian Gulf. A complete summary of the development of the Abrams would fill many pages, as would the story of its deployments around the globe – but that is not the purpose of this book. Rather, this book concerns the Abrams tankers who have waged war in the Middle East.

The U.S. Army developed the MBT-70 to replace the M60 MBT. Although 14 pilots, including number two seen here, were built, cost overruns and delays in development induced Congress to terminate funding for the MBT-70 project in 1971.

Following the shutdown of the MBT-70 program, the army initiated development of a new prototype main battle tank, the XM1. Chrysler's version was chosen over one produced by General Motors. Seen here is the ninth pilot vehicle out of the 11 built.

An XM1 pilot vehicle is run through its paces at Ft. Knox, Kentucky. After Chrysler won the competition to produce the contract for this tank in late 1976, rigorous developmental and operational tests were conducted on the pilot vehicles at several test grounds until 1981.

Dust coats the rear end of an M1 during a firing exercise. The design of the rear of the turret distinguishes this vehicle as an M1, with the characteristic sloping facet on which the crosswind sensor, radio antenna mounts, and two spare track links are positioned.

The first production M1 MBT left the Lima Tank Plant in Ohio in late February 1980, christened the Abrams after Gen. Creighton Abrams. The example in this photo was M1 number one, named "Thunderbolt" after Gen. Abrams's Sherman tank in World War II.

M1 Abrams Specifications

Weight:	67.6 tons
Length Gun forward:	32.04 feet
Hull length:	26.02 feet
Width:	12 feet
Height:	8 feet
Crew:	4 (commander, gunner, loader, driver)
Main armament:	105mm L52 M68 rifled cannon (M1) 120mm L44 M256 smoothbore cannon (M1A1, M1A2, M1A2SEP) with 42 rounds
Secondary armament:	1 x .50-caliber (12.7mm) M2HB machine gun with 900 rounds 2 x 7.62mm M240 machine guns with 8,800 rounds
Engine:	AGT1500C multi-fuel turbine engine
Power/weight ratio:	24.5 h.p./metric ton (18.27 kW/t)
Transmission:	Allison DDA X-1100-3B
Suspension:	Torsion bar
Ground clearance:	19 inches (M1, M1A1) 18 inches (M1A2)
Fuel capacity:	500 gallons
Range:	300 miles
Speed, governed:	Road: 45 m.p.h. - Off-road: 33 m.p.h.

The turret of an M1 is traversed toward the left during tests of the tank. The Avco Lycoming AGT-1500 turbine engine required a massive amount of air, and extensive air filters were necessary to deal with dust such as has been churned up on this test ground.

An identifying characteristic of the M1 that differentiated it from the XM1 was the long, tubular flash suppressor for the 7.62mm coaxial machine gun positioned to the right front of the 105mm gun shield. Toward the rear of the hull is stenciled in black "C13."

An ammunition specialist with the patch of the 1st Cavalry Division "First Team" lifts a 105mm armor-piercing, discarding-sabot (APDS) round, to be used in an M-1 Abrams main battle tank during Operation Desert Shield. The black-colored sabot flies off when the projectile is fired. Yellow caution stickers are on the projectiles.

The M1A1 Abrams saw the main gun change from a 105mm rifle to a 120mm smoothbore. The shells seen here in the foreground are steel-cased 105mm Target Practice Discarding Sabot-Tracer (TPDS-T).

GIs secure M1 tanks to flatcars during Exercise Reforger '85. Reforger was an annual exercise conducted in the Cold War by NATO to test its readiness to deploy quickly to West Germany in the event of war with the Warsaw Pact.

During Reforger '85 on 1 January 1985, an M88A1 armored recovery vehicle, left, aids an M1 Abrams, wearing the flat-medium-green early camouflage scheme. An amber flashing convoy warning light is stowed on the rail adjacent to the smoke discharger.

In February 2001 an M1A1 Abrams MBT pauses at an engineer observation post. The tank is painted in a woodland camouflage scheme and is marked KFOR, which stands for Kosovo Force, a NATO-led military force operating under a United Nations mandate, charged with restoring peace to war-torn Kosovo.

At Ft. Stewart, Georgia, two tank crewmen of A Company, 1st Battalion, 64th Armor Regiment, 24th Infantry Division, have swung open the front right skirt section of their M1A1 tank in order to adjust tread fittings. They were preparing to deploy to Saudi Arabia in 1990.

An M1A1 presents a ghostly image in a sandstorm during the 1990-1991 First Gulf War. Conditions such as these proved challenging for crewmen and equipment, testing to the ultimate the ability of the vehicle's crew and engine air filtration systems.

The Desert Sand camouflage of this M1A1 photographed during operations to liberate Kuwait in 1990-1991 makes the vehicle blend in well with the dusty, sandy terrain. Marked in black on one of the side skirts are the troop designation, G, and vehicle number, 4.

At a camp in Saudi Arabia during Operation Desert Shield, M1A1 Abrams main battle tanks of A Company, 3rd Battalion, 32nd Armor Regiment, 1st Cavalry Division prepare to conduct live-firing practice in preparation for the liberation of Kuwait.

During Operation Desert Shield in 1990, the M1A1 to the left apparently has thrown its left track, and the M1A1 to the rear of it is preparing to push it. Both tanks have tactical signs of the type employed by the 3rd Armored Cavalry Regiment.

Captain William V. Hill's M1A1 Abrams command tank, G-66, of G Troop, 2nd Squadron, 3rd Armored Cavalry Regiment, is shrouded in early morning-fog in Saudi Arabia in 1990. To the left is a FIST-V crewed by artillery forward observers.

During the First Gulf War, an M1A1 lays a smoke screen. This was accomplished with the vehicle-engine-exhaust smoke system (VEESS), which sprayed fuel into the exhaust gasses, creating a dense vapor. The VEESS was discontinued in the early 1990s.

A mine-clearing blade is on the front end of a 3rd ACR M1A1 during the First Gulf War. The top pieces of the Mine Clearing Blade, a.k.a. Track Width Mine Plow (TWMP) lie flat until plowing begins. The plow unearths and shoves aside any mines encountered.

Crewmen look over a mine blade in the raised position on an M1A1. To the left of the soldier in the parka are the front ends of the two skids that rode on the surface of the ground when the blade was lowered into the earth. The turret is traversed to the rear.

Artwork for *Stupendous Daman* is viewed on an M1A1 of the 1st Platoon, H, Troop, 2nd Squadron, 3rd Armored Cavalry Regiment during the First Gulf War. There was time aplenty for such artistic creations during the buildup for Operation Desert Storm.

The left front of an M1A1 of the 3rd Platoon, H Troop, 2nd Squadron, 3rd Armored Cavalry Regiment, during the First Gulf War shows a painting of a muscle man wearing sunglasses and the crew step made of a piece of cable at the bottom of the skirt.

Iraqi armor was not much of a match for the M1A1 during the First Gulf War. Often, tanks such as this T55 or derivative were placed hull-down in entrenchments, where they lacked even the benefit of mobility, becoming sitting ducks for the Coalition forces.

During the First Gulf War, a group including Col. Douglas H. Starr, commander of the 3rd Armored Cavalry Regiment, gathers next to M1A1 F2 of F Troop of that regiment. A rack installed on the side of the turret holds rations boxes and liquid containers.

A gunner inside the XM1 Abrams tank checks the vehicle's fire control system. The 105mm M68 gun of the XM1 and M1 featured this oval-shaped breech while the later 120mm M256 breech block is square.

M1A1 Abrams MBTs assigned to the 3rd Squadron, 7th Cavalry, 3rd Infantry Division, are secured with chains to railroad flatcars for delivery from Fort Stewart, Georgia, to Savannah, Georgia, on 10 September 1996. Soft covers are on the tail-light assemblies.

An M1A1 of the 1st Tank Battalion, 1st Marine Division, uses a mine blade, fully lowered into the sand, to breach the obstacle belt on a landing beach. The Marines began transitioning from their M60A1 tanks to the M1A1 in 1990, acquiring 269 by 1991.

In addition to the mine-clearing blade, the Abrams main battle tank also could be fitted with a track-width mine-clearing roller, as seen in this photo of an M1A1 of the 3rd Armored Calvary Regiment at Fort Polk, Louisiana, during exercises in the late 1990s.

M1 Development

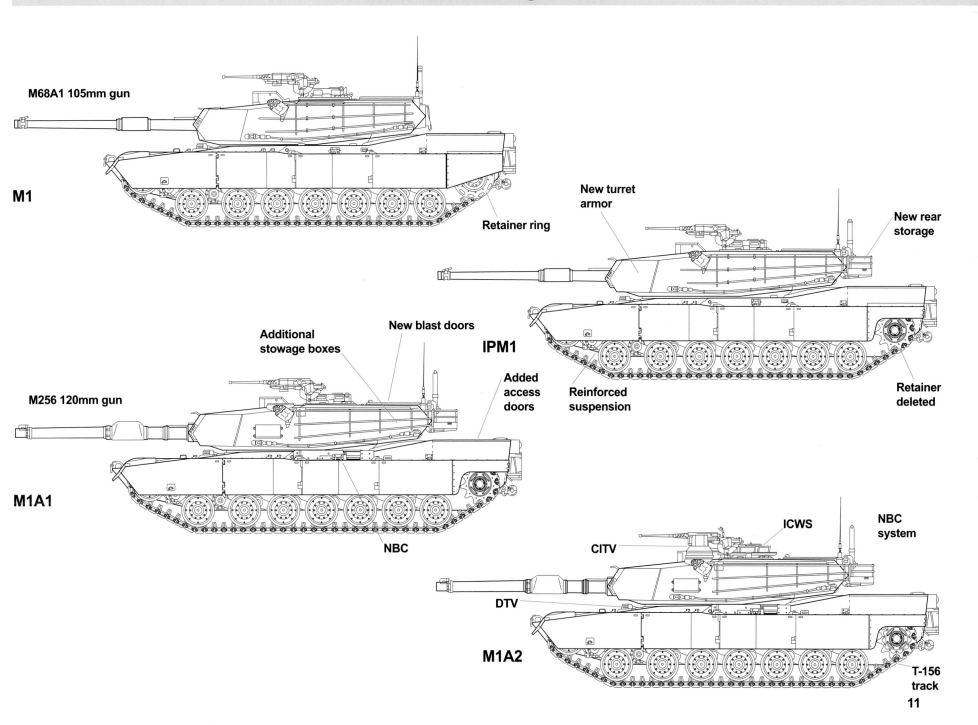

M68A1 105mm gun

M1

Retainer ring

New turret armor

New rear storage

IPM1

Additional stowage boxes

New blast doors

Added access doors

M256 120mm gun

Reinforced suspension

Retainer deleted

M1A1

NBC

ICWS

NBC system

CITV

DTV

M1A2

T-156 track

A crewman sits on the roof of the turret of a USMC M1A1, registration number 584399, during exercises at the Marine Corps Air-Ground Combat Center, Twentynine Palms, California, in February 2000. "Highlander" is stenciled in black on the bore evacuator on the 120mm gun. On the left side of the rear of the turret bustle is an External Auxiliary Power Unit (EAPU), a feature added to the M1A1 and its submodels as well as the M1A2 (but not the M1A2 SEP) in the mid-1990s. It has several forest green replacement roadwheels and is painted CARC (Chemical Agent Resistant Coating) Sand.

Marine M1A1s prepare to engage in target practice during Exercise Iron Magic at Al Hamra Training Area in the United Arab Emirates in November 2000. Visible below the machine gun on each turret is the commander's independent thermal viewer (CITV).

M1A1s of the 2nd Tank Battalion, 2nd Marine Division, participate in a combined-arms exercise at Twentynine Palms in February 2000. The two green side-skirt panels were replacement parts that had not yet been painted in Desert Sand.

A USMC M1A2 at the Al Hamra Training Area in November 2000 sports the name "Jail Bait" stenciled on the bore evacuator of the main gun. Stenciled in black on the smoke grenade stowage box below the eight-shot M257 smoke-grenade launcher is "D32."

United States flags flying, M1A1 Main Battle Tanks of the 3d ACR tanks engage in live-fire maneuvers at Mubârak Military City, Egypt, during Exercise Bright Star 01/02, a joint operation of U.S., Spanish, and Egyptian military units.

An M1A2 fires a round during a training exercise at Udari Range in Kuwait in 2003. The Abrams is home stationed in the Marine Corps Air Ground Combat Center (MCAGCC) at Twentynine Palms, California, and belongs to the 3rd Platoon, D Co, 1st Tank Battalion, and assigned to BLT 1/1, 13th MEU. The three black rings near the muzzle of the 120mm gun barrel and three dashes inside open end of Vee denote 3rd Platoon. Vee pointed to right or 9 o'clock is tactical mark of Delta Company.

A Grim Reaper, 3rd Platoon logo is stenciled on the smoke grenade storage box on the side of the turret of this Abrams, undergoing live-fire training at Udari Range in Kuwait in December 2003.

A rear view of the same M1A2 seen in the preceding photo shows the fitting for the exhaust tower of the deep-water fording kit (DWFK) installed over the engine exhaust grille. Using the DWFK, the M1A2 can drive through water up to 7.5 feet deep.

A USMC M1A2 is being offloaded from a landing craft, air cushioned (LCAC) from the USS *Tarawa* (LHA-1) Amphibious Ready Group in 2003. Stenciled on the bore extractor is "Cannibal," and "C32" is on the front of the left fender.

A soldier is guiding an M1A2 of the 1st Squadron, 10th Cavalry Regiment, 4th Infantry Division, onto the ramp from the military transport ship Cape Victory at Port Shu'aiba, Kuwait, on 3 April 2003 in support of Operation Iraqi Freedom, or the Second Gulf War.

The center tank in this group of M1A2s operating in the desert has just fired a round, and its commander is observing the effect of the fire. An observer is also on the roof of the Abrams to the left. The center and left tanks have the code E2 on their skirts.

The code E2 is on the side skirts of this advancing M1A2 indicates the vehicle is E Troop, 2nd Platoon, 2nd Squadron, 3 ACR. Visible on the roof of the turret is the head of the commander's independent thermal viewer (CITV).

Mechanics lower a powerpack into an Abrams of the 1st Tank Battalion, USMC, in Kuwait in 2003. Above the transmission, from left to right are the engine oil cooler, primary transmission oil cooler, engine exhaust, and auxiliary transmission oil cooler.

In another view of the same Abrams, the M88 armored recovery vehicle that is lowering the powerpack is visible. Designed to be quickly removed or replaced, the powerpack included the engine, transmission, final drives, and cooling system.

An M1A2, code E2, of the 2nd Squadron, 3rd Armored Cavalry Regiment, undergoes refueling from an M978 HEMTT northeast of al-Fallûjah, Iraq, during Operation Iraqi Freedom on 29 August 2003. To the right is an M88 recovery vehicle.

A close-up view shows the crew at work refueling the M1A2. The fuel capacity of Abrams models from the M1 to the M1A2 is 505 gallons distributed in four fuel tanks. On the other hand, the M1A2 SEP carries 445.4 gallons in three fuel tanks.

During Operation Iraqi Freedom in 2003, Iraqi forces were ill-suited to contend with the U.S. and Coalition forces invading the country. This knocked-out Iraqi T-72M1 is typical of the swath of destruction the Abrams spread as the army advanced on Baghdâd.

M1A1s of the 63rd Armor Regiment, 1st Infantry Division, provide support for infantrymen in Kirkûk, Iraq, in April 2003. The turrets are heavily laden with packs. The name on the 120mm gun barrel of the first tank appears to be "Excellent Choice."

An M1A1 Abrams MBT of C Company, 1st Battalion, 37th Armor Regiment, of the 1st Brigade, 1st Armored Division, has just finished a sweep of a market Iraq, on 4 September 2003. The unit markings are on white panels on the front of the hull.

Abrams M1A2s of G Troop, 3rd Cavalry Regiment were photographed on a highway during Operation Iraqi Freedom. The lead vehicle has the code G2 on its side skirts. On both tanks the commander's independent thermal viewer is prominent on the turret roof.

On 13 November 2003, the crew of an M1A1 Abrams main battle tank commanded by Capt. William T. Cundy (standing behind the .50-caliber machine gun in the commander's weapon station, or CWS) conducts a combat patrol in Baghdâd, Iraq. The A-65 bumper number on denotes A Company and the 65 is the XO's tank. The unit markings on the front of the hull indicate that the tank was assigned to A Company, Task Force 1st Battalion, 35th Armor Regiment, 1st Armored Division. The driver is buttoned-up in his compartment, his hatch closed, and he is using his periscopes and instructions from the commander as guides for driving the vehicle. To the front of the CWS is the "doghouse," the armored cover of the gunner's primary sight, or GPS. The sand colored box, to the left of the Gunner's Primary Sight, is the Blue Force Tracker (BFT) system antenna. The BFT shows the positions of enemy forces, friendly units, and obstacles, overlaid on computer generated map to provide better situational awareness for the tank crew. On each side of the turret is a smoke-grenade discharger, equipped with a canvas cover to keep out dust and foreign objects. Visible on the right front facet of the turret (to the left of the main gun in the photo) are L-shaped Velcro attachments for mounting a combat-identification panel (CIP). On the left front facet of the turret, a CIP is installed on the Velcro fittings. On the left rear of the turret, an opened cardboard meals-ready-to-eat (MRE) rations box with the distinctive crescent symbol visible on it.

In a photo taken at the same site as the photograph at the lower right of the preceding page, an M1A2 of G Troop, 3rd Cavalry Regiment, moves among civilian traffic during Operation Iraqi Freedom. On each side of the front of the turret is a combat identification panel (CIP) of the flat type.

Crewmen survey a disabled 2nd Brigade Combat Team, 3rd Infantry Division M1A1 prior to recovery efforts. The rear of the turret is in the foreground, showing the external auxiliary power unit on the left and, rising next to it, the crosswind sensor, which feeds crosswind data into the fire-control electronics unit.

In another view of the same M1A1, the left track is in a shambles, and the left fender and skirts are missing. Louver-like combat identification panels (CIPs) on the sides and rear of the turret help prevent friendly forces from targeting the tank using thermal sights.

The CIP on the left side of the turret of the disabled M1A1 is marked "this side off." These panels are reversible, the "on" side being the one with thermal-reflective surface and the "off" side bring painted with chemical agent resistant coating (CARC).

An overall view of the same disabled M1A1 provides a better sense of the tank's position off the road and the nature of the stricken vehicle's predicament. A tow cable has been secured to the left front of its hull, and an attempt will soon be made to recover it.

An M88 recovery vehicle has begun to extricate the same disabled M1A1 from the soft ground along the road. The tank's left track is off. The lid of the stowage box on the side of the turret is open. In the background, another M1A1 is in a covering position.

The disabled M1A1 is viewed from its front right corner. The object next to the driver's hatch is a sledgehammer. Bloody rags next to the smoke-grenade dischargers attest to the fact that at least one crewman was wounded when this M1A1 was disabled.

The turret has been blown off the hull of this M1A1; the rear of the turret is next to the rear of the tank, and an external auxiliary power unit is visible on top of the turret bustle. Pioneer tools are visible inside the bin on top of the hull next to the opening for the turret.

The turret blown off the M1A1 in the preceding photo is seen where it crashed into the ground. Panels atop the turret bustle blew off as designed, in order to vent the force of the explosion of the 120mm ammunition upward. In the foreground is an ammunition rack.

Soldiers survey the turret blown off the M1A1. On the loader's machine gun mount on the left side of the turret is a Transparent Armor Gun Shield or TAGS. The commander's and the loader's machine guns have been dismounted.

In a close-up view of a disabled Abrams MBT, the front right bogie assembly is detached from the hull, showing the torsion bar for the front bogie assembly on the left side of the hull. To the right is the suspension arm for the right compensating idler wheel.

Inside the well deck of USS *Saipan* (LHA-2) in March 2004, an Abrams assigned to the 24th Marine Expeditionary Unit is being driven off a landing craft utility of Amphibious Craft Unit 2. At the rear of the hull is the exhaust tower of the deep-water fording kit.

An M1A1 of Bravo Troop, 1st Battalion, 4th Cavalry Regiment, has an extra stowage box secured to the rails on the right side of the turret. On the front left corner of the turret roof is a spare drive-sprocket ring with a spare bogie wheel fastened on top of it.

The crew of an Abrams nicknamed *Ali Baba & the 3 Thieves,* assigned to 2nd Battalion, 63rd Armor Regiment, 3rd Brigade Combat Team, 1st Infantry Division, returns to base after a series of engagements with insurgents at Ba'qûbah, Iraq.

An M1A1 of Bravo Company,1st Battalion, 185th Armor Regiment, part of TF Tacoma, skirts a canal while on anti-insurgent reconnaissance near Balad, Iraq, on 6 September 2004. Commander and the loader are ready to lay down machine gun fire if required.

An Abrams MBT with an External Auxiliary Power Unit (EAPU) inside the turret bustle rack takes up position during a mortar assault by insurgents in al-Fallûjah, Iraq, on 14 August 2004. In order to gain back the lost stowage area it is equipped with a Bustle Rack Extension (BRE). Each end of the BRE can hold a five-gallon jug, usually of water or oil. This tank is attached to the 1st Marine Division, which is here conducting security and stabilization operations in western Iraq's al-Anbâr Province.

In late October 2004 a well-weathered M1A1 of Bravo Troop, 1st Battalion, 4th Armored Cavalry Regiment, 1st Infantry Division, departs from Forward Operating Base MacKenzie, about 96km north of Baghdâd, in Iraq. The vehicle's unit code is stenciled on light-colored panels on a tow bar attached to the front of the hull. The violet and orange coloration of the glass on the driver's periscope is caused by a treatment that prevents the driver from being blinded by laser light.

D32 is on the front of each fender of this M1A1 of the 11th Marine Expeditionary Unit, Special Operations Capable, in an-Najaf for a raid on the Mahdî Army in August 2004.

Iraqi small arms fire punctured SFC2 (Supplemental Fuel Carrying) bladders mounted on the side of the turret, causing fuel to spill into the air cleaners or "Vee" packs and causing the engine to abort and not restart. The Abrams crew then destroyed the disabled tank in place, to prevent it from being captured.

An Abrams MBT of Alpha Troop, 1st Battalion, 4th Cavalry Regiment, stands guard at an intersection in ad-Dulû'îyah, Iraq, on 18 October 2004. A tow bar is mounted on the front of the hull for fast deployment if needed, and the right fender is missing.

It is reported that no Abrams MBTs were destroyed by single, knockout hits during the Second Gulf War, but several were destroyed as a result of spreading fires, and others were disabled and then scuttled to prevent their falling into enemy hands.

This M1A1 was deeply mired near Sayyid 'Abd, Iraq, during Operation Iraqi Freedom. The marking on the turret indicates it belonged to Bravo Company, 2nd Battalion, but its regiment is not identified. Areas of soft, wet ground were a hazard for tanks in Iraq.

An M1A1 photographed during operations near al-Fallûjah in May 2004 lacks any visible markings. The M257 smoke-grenade dischargers on the side of the turret, with eight individual tubes, replaced the M250 discharger, a one-piece aluminum casting.

An M1A2 is partially in view in a scene of fighting during Operation Iraqi Freedom. On the rear of the hull are rolls of concertina wire, which would be strung on posts around the tank when it was laagered (encamped) for the night, to defend against infiltrators.

Crewmen of an M1A1 of Charlie Company, 1st Battalion, 3rd Marines, 1st Marine Division, watch for signs of trouble during Operation Al-Fajr, or the Second Battle of al-Fallûjah, in late 2004. There are no visible markings on this M1A1 Abrams.

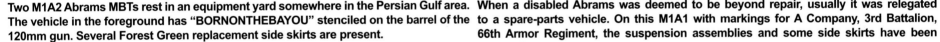

Two M1A2 Abrams MBTs rest in an equipment yard somewhere in the Persian Gulf area. The vehicle in the foreground has "BORNONTHEBAYOU" stenciled on the barrel of the 120mm gun. Several Forest Green replacement side skirts are present.

The M1A1 shown in the preceding photograph is viewed from the right side. Spare bogie wheels are still stored on the side of the turret-bustle rack and on the front of the turret roof, and the right drive sprocket has not been removed with the rest of the suspension.

When a disabled Abrams was deemed to be beyond repair, usually it was relegated to a spare-parts vehicle. On this M1A1 with markings for A Company, 3rd Battalion, 66th Armor Regiment, the suspension assemblies and some side skirts have been removed.

An M1A2 undergoes engine repairs in a maintenance yard. A crane boom is poised over the rear deck, and several access doors on the deck are open. Marked on the side skirts are the number 222 and a rearward-pointing identification chevron.

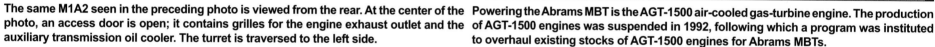

The same M1A2 seen in the preceding photo is viewed from the rear. At the center of the photo, an access door is open; it contains grilles for the engine exhaust outlet and the auxiliary transmission oil cooler. The turret is traversed to the left side.

Powering the Abrams MBT is the AGT-1500 air-cooled gas-turbine engine. The production of AGT-1500 engines was suspended in 1992, following which a program was instituted to overhaul existing stocks of AGT-1500 engines for Abrams MBTs.

The AGT-1500 engine is viewed from another angle. At the bottom of the photo is a canvas cover, which keeps dust out of the aperture for the low-pressure compressor. The AGT-1500 originally was made by Avco Lycoming and later by Honeywell.

The 120mm main gun and coaxial machine gun flash suppressor of this M1A1 of the 3rd Battalion 69th Armor, 1st BCT, 3ID have been removed. Stenciled in black on the front of the turret is the black panther symbol of the regiment.

During a firefight in al-Fallûjah, Iraq, on 10 December 2004, the 120mm main gun of an M1A1 of the Marines' 2nd Tank Battalion blasts a building containing insurgents who had been firing at the Marines. The savage force of the 120mm gun fired at point-blank range is apparent. On top of the turret roof is a blue and white civilian-type cooler. The individual tubes of the left M257 smoke-grenade dischargers are visible on the side of the turret.

Two U.S. Marine Corps M1A1 Abrams MBTs assigned to Bravo Company, 1st Battalion 8th Marine Regiment, 1st Marine Division, let loose with their 120mm main guns at suspected insurgent strongholds in al-Fallûjah, Iraq, while participating in a security and stabilization operation (SASO) carried out during Operation Iraqi Freedom. The name on the bore evacuator of the closer tank is "Maximus," while that on the other tank is "Lion-Heart." The farther tank's main gun is painted green, with a sand-colored bore evacuator.

An M1A1 of the Tank Platoon, Battalion Landing Team 1st Battalion, 4th Marines, 11th Marine Expeditionary Unit (Special Operations Capable) engages in a training exercise in an-Najaf Province, Iraq, in January 2005. Fitted over the exhaust outlet on the rear of the hull is the elbow-shaped fitting for the deep-water fording kit exhaust tower stowed atop the turret bustle. Two shorter towers were also provided for the engine air intakes.

At the Rodriguez Live Fire Complex, Republic of Korea, in 2005 a 120mm projectile can be seen speeding downrange from an M1A1. During training, a cost-saving practice round with a tracer element is often used.

An M1A1 of the 1st Battalion, 185th Armor Regiment speeds to the aid of friendly forces at the Yarmûk traffic circle in Mosul, Iraq, on 2 January 2005. This traffic circle had been a prime area for attacks by insurgents ever since the November 2004 Battle of Mosul.

An M1A2 churns up dust during a mission in support of Operation Iraqi Freedom. The dusty conditions posed a constant challenge to the crews of Abrams tanks, whose gas turbine engines required massive amounts of clean, filtered air in order to function.

"ERICA FIRE" is the name stenciled on the bore evacuator of the 120mm gun of this M1A2 standing watch. The .50-caliber machine gun mount of the commander's weapon station is the late type, which rotates on a ring around the perimeter of the fixed cupola.

U.S. Army vehicles are coming through a road barrier, possibly heading out on patrol or on an anti-insurgent mission. In the foreground are an M113-type vehicle and, just behind it, a Bradley fighting vehicle. To the right are several Abrams main battle tanks.

The Abrams MBT to the right is using a tow bar to recover an M1A2 that has suffered a breakdown. When an armored recovery vehicle was not readily available, an Abrams MBT could serve as a makeshift tow vehicle for a reasonable distance.

An M1A1 charges forward in a village setting. A combat identification panel is affixed to the side of the turret to the immediate rear of the commander's weapon station, and the identification code E2 is applied in large figures on one of the side-skirt panels. The vehicle belongs to the 3rd Armored Cavalry Regiment, 2nd Platoon, Echo Troop.

An Abrams MBT is maneuvering onto or off of a transporter trailer in the desert. It is painted overall sand with the exception of the smoke-grenade box on the turret. The nickname "MESCAL" is stenciled in black on the 120mm gun barrel of the tank, which belongs to the 3rd Armored Cavalry Regiment, Mike Company, 3rd Platoon.

The commander's independent thermal viewer, an identifying feature of the M1A2, is toward the front of the turret roof on this Abrams parked next to a pillbox. "L2" is inscribed on two side-skirt panels that appear to be a slightly different color than the other panels.

Among other vehicles, two M1A2s are secured to trailers at a marshalling yard in the desert. On the roof of the turret of the closest tank are helmets, ballistic vests, and personal weapons and gear. "Dixon Here" is stenciled on the 120mm gun barrel.

Even the all-terrain HMMWV could become mired in the soft ground occasionally encountered in Iraq, and an M1A2 was more than able to pull it free. Although the tank's unit markings are not visible, "Adrenaline Rush" on the 120mm barrel is.

A soldier fastens a tow cable to the eye at the upper left rear of the hull of an M1A2 mired in soft ground. The green smoke-grenade stowage box and rear skirt panels are replacement parts. Parts come in either Sand or Green colors, depending what part number is used when ordered or what color is in stock

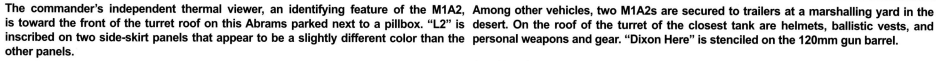

The same M1A2 shown in the preceding photo is viewed from the right side, mired to the top of the hull. A significant pitfall for the heavy Abrams tanks in the Mesopotamian Plain of Iraq was the prevalence of deep soil, which could virtually swallow a tank.

Another shot of the same mired M1A2 shows that the front of the hull is firmly planted in the ground. Another Abrams stands watch in the background, and adjacent to that tank is an M88 armored recovery vehicle, which will attempt to extricate the mired M1A2.

In addition to soft ground, gullies and man-made ditches would also disable an Abrams. This M1A2 went sideways into a V-shaped gully, firmly immobilizing it. The left fender has either been raised or pushed open. The identification code D2 is on the side skirts.

A tow bar is stored in brackets normally found on the rear of a M88A1 recovery vehicle, on the side of the M1A2 hull. Painted on the 120mm gun barrel is *Dickens Cider.* A tow chain has been secured to a clevis on the rear of the hull preparatory to recovery.

The "dog bone" is dangling by chains below the center of the plow on an M1A2 nicknamed *Dixon Mere*. These plows feature different designs of dog bones. This one is flared at each end like a true dog bone. Others are larger and are cylindrical in shape.

Soldiers from Bravo Company, 1st Battalion, 30th Infantry, 3rd Brigade Combat Team, 3rd Infantry Division, scramble into position on their M1A1s at a base at Ba'qûbah, Iraq, on 27 May 2005. They are about to set out on a mission.

At Camp 'Arifjân, Kuwait, on 2 March 2005, Operations Specialist 2nd Class Alex Ponce, right, a U.S. Navy Reservist, inspects a U.S. Army M1A1 Abrams main battle tank for the U.S. Navy Customs Inspection Battalion. A group of tanks was being cleared for shipment back to the United States after serving in operations in Iraq. The Naval Expeditionary Logistics Support Force (NAVELSF), Forward Oscar, Charlie Company was performing the customs mission for the U.S. Army throughout Kuwait and Iraq at this time.

Three crewmen wearing ballistic vests stand atop an M1A2 in Iraq. Gear piled on top of the turret bustle includes the seemingly ubiquitous plastic civilian-type cooler. A tow bar is stowed on the side of the hull, and a combat-identification panel is on the turret.

Morale is high with these M1A2 crewmen, who are smiling and laughing. Fastened to the forward end of the rails on the side of the turret is a spare drive-sprocket ring. A close examination of the photo reveals that the loader's machine gun has a shield.

Stenciled on the 120mm gun barrel of this M1A2 is "Intentionally Left Blank." The main gun on the M1A2 was the same one used in the M1A1: the M256 120mm gun. To the right of the right tail light assembly is stenciled in small figures "I-22," and "I-22" is also marked in large figures on the side skirts. The single-piece-casting M250 smoke-grenade dischargers are present on this vehicle

Abrams MBT crewmen take a break from operations at a camp. The external machine guns have been dismounted, and the men are getting their equipment in order. The code M1 is on the side skirts of the tank to the left, while the one to the right lacks a code.

On this 3/3ACR M1A2, the ballistic shield is present on the loader's machine gun mount. For extra protection to the exposed commander and loader, several sand bags are piled up between the CITV and the gunner's primary sight cover.

A good view of the upper surfaces of the front of the hull and the turret of an M1A2 are available in this photo. The armored doors of the ballistic shield of the gunner's primary sight are open. This structure is sometimes referred to as the "doghouse."

The commander's weapon station (CWS) of an M1A2 is viewed close-up. Whereas the CWS of M1A1 and earlier models allowed the commander to fire a .50-caliber machine gun from inside the turret, this version requires that he fire with his upper body exposed.

Sergeant 1st Class Eric Pearrow, an Abrams commander of the 3 Squadron, 3rd Armored Cavalry Regiment, poses in front of his tank. Sergeant Pearrow was killed in Baghdâd on 24 November 2005 when his M1A2 accidentally rolled over into a canal and he drowned.

The M1A2 with the green replacement fender at the center of the photo appears to be the same one in the preceding photo. A tow bar has been attached to the front end, and the front side skirts have been opened; they are casting a shadow on the ground by the tank.

Sergeant First Class Altman stands next to a disabled Abrams. The right track and fender are missing. A ratchet strap holds the front side skirt shut. The turret is traversed to the rear, showing spare track links and bogie wheel painted Desert Sand.

At Camp Striker in Iraq in April 2005, members of 2nd Platoon, Apache Troop, 3rd Armored Cavalry Regiment carry out maintenance on their Abrams MBTs. The barrel of "Adrenaline Rush" is in the foreground; at the center is "American Muscle," an M1A2.

A U.S. Marine Corps M1A1 Abrams MBT approaches the front gate of Camp Hadîthah, Iraq, on 19 April 2005. The dark discoloration typically found on the engine-exhaust grille at the center rear of the hull is visible. A tow bar is stowed atop the turret bustle.

Marines at Camp Buehring, Kuwait, perform engine maintenance during a sandstorm on 9 June 2005. To the right is 1st. Lt. Jose L. Castillo, commander of the Tank Platoon, Battalion Landing Team, 2nd Battalion, 8th Marine Regiment, 26th MEU (SOC).

An Abrams M1A2 Main Battle tank assigned to D Company, 3rd Armored Cavalry Regiment, bears a black dragon insignia on the front facet of the turret. Unit coding visible from this side consists solely of the letter D on the side skirt. The tank was painted overall in a sand camouflage. The stowage box on the side of the turret was a light gray color. A spare bogie wheel was stowed on the turret roof to the front of the CITV. An Armored Cavalry Squadron was organized with three Cavalry Troops (13 Bradleys, nine Tanks, two Mortar tracks), a Tank Company (14 Tanks) and a Howitzer Battery (six M109A6s).

An M1A1 of the 2nd Tank Battalion, 2nd Marine Regiment, provides area security at a street intersection in al-Fallûjah, Iraq, supporting personnel of Weapons Company, 1st Battalion, 6th Marine Regiment. The rear side-skirt panel has been removed from this vehicle, and a tow bar is secured alongside the stowage box on the side of the turret. The commander has turned his weapon station to the rear, so his hatch cover provides him with frontal protection.

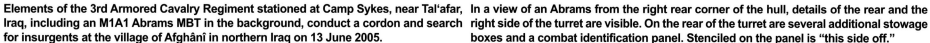

Elements of the 3rd Armored Cavalry Regiment stationed at Camp Sykes, near Tal'afar, Iraq, including an M1A1 Abrams MBT in the background, conduct a cordon and search for insurgents at the village of Afghânî in northern Iraq on 13 June 2005.

On this M1A2 in position near an Iraqi highway, the M2 unit code and the inscription "Maddog" and accompanying art indicate the tank belongs to M, or Mad Dog, Company. Small, stenciled figures at the bottom of the front skirt are the DoD shipping number.

In a view of an Abrams from the right rear corner of the hull, details of the rear and the right side of the turret are visible. On the rear of the turret are several additional stowage boxes and a combat identification panel. Stenciled on the panel is "this side off."

Two crewmen enjoy the sun on the turret of their M1A2. Piled on the turret roof is an assortment of gear, including what appears to be a large white ice chest. On the rear of the hull are two rolls of concertina wire, and a tow bar is stowed on the side of the hull.

This photograph and the following two depict an M1A2 with the name "Deez" stenciled on the barrel of the 120mm gun. On the side skirts is a very faded or dust-covered code, D3. Behind the CITV is a shield for the loader's machine gun.

On the front of the turret, the combat identification panels typically seen on Abrams MBTs in Iraq are not present. A better view is provided of the shield on the loader's machine gun mount. The top stowage rail on the side of the turret is bent.

The M1A2 named "Deez" is viewed from the left rear corner. The first letter of the name of an armored cavalry Abrams corresponds to the troop designation. Thus, "Deez" and the unit code of this tank, D3, indicate that it was assigned to D, or Dragon, Troop.

"Disturbed Individuals" is stenciled on the 120mm gun barrel of a 3rd Armored Cavalry Regiment M1A1. Three black rings on the bore evacuator indicate it is the third vehicle in the platoon, and the code D1 on the skirts indicates the 1st Platoon, Dragon Troop.

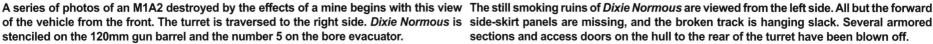

A series of photos of an M1A2 destroyed by the effects of a mine begins with this view of the vehicle from the front. The turret is traversed to the right side. *Dixie Normous* is stenciled on the 120mm gun barrel and the number 5 on the bore evacuator.

Dixie Normous is viewed from a position a bit closer to the vehicle than in the preceding view, showing the gaping hole in the rear of the turret and the breech of the 120mm gun. The round loader's hatch is poised open at the top of the turret.

The still smoking ruins of *Dixie Normous* are viewed from the left side. All but the forward side-skirt panels are missing, and the broken track is hanging slack. Several armored sections and access doors on the hull to the rear of the turret have been blown off.

Below the side skirt of *Dixie Normous* are puddles of molten aluminum from the road wheels. A steel cable step is at the bottom of the skirt. Recessed in the skirt is a latch for securing the skirt to the skirt bracket.

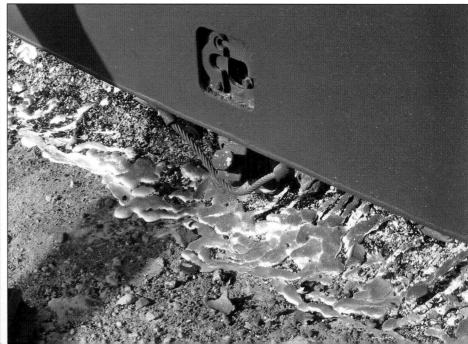

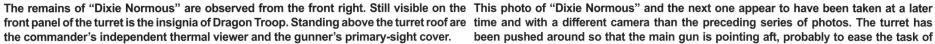

The remains of "Dixie Normous" are observed from the front right. Still visible on the front panel of the turret is the insignia of Dragon Troop. Standing above the turret roof are the commander's independent thermal viewer and the gunner's primary-sight cover.

A soldier looks over the devastation inflicted on "Dixie Normous." Most of the turret bustle has been blown off; a section of the bustle still adheres to the left side of the turret. The driver's hatch is open, and the hatch cover is swung to the right side of the hatch.

This photo of "Dixie Normous" and the next one appear to have been taken at a later time and with a different camera than the preceding series of photos. The turret has been pushed around so that the main gun is pointing aft, probably to ease the task of recovery.

The area where the turret bustle used to be on "Dixie Normous" is viewed from the rear. To the far left is the left side of the bustle. The right sliding door of the ammunition compartment in the bustle is still in place; the right sliding door is missing.

A trooper rigs a hoist cable to a 3rd Armored Cavalry Regiment M1A2 with a Dragon Troop insignia on the front of the turret. The hoist cable is routed to the boom of the vehicle standing by to the left, an M88A2 Hercules armored recovery vehicle.

The M1A2 is now resting on the M1000 semi-trailer, and the extent of the damage of the suspension, apparently caused by a mine, is apparent. The soldier in the foreground is hefting a clevis, and a tow cable is secured to another clevis on the front of the hull.

With an M88A2 Hercules supporting the M1A2 from each side, the disabled tank is lowered onto an M1000 heavy equipment transporter semi-trailer. The M1000 is the semi-trailer component of the Heavy Equipment Transport System (HETS), the other part of which is the Oshkosh M1070 truck tractor. The HETS has an off-road capability and was designed primarily to transport Abrams tanks and has a capacity of up to 70 tons. The M1000 semi-trailer has a load-leveling hydraulic suspension and automatically steerable axles.

The M1A2 to the left is disabled and is undergoing recovery by the two M88A2s to the right. The M88A2 nearest to the M1A1 is pulling on the tank with a drag line routed through a large snatch block, in order to compound the pulling power of the winch.

The M1A2 has now been pulled closer to the recovery vehicles, and the M88A2 with the raised boom now has a taut drag line running from its winch to the tank. This Abrams was the third tank in 2nd Platoon, Dragon Troop, 2nd Armored Cavalry Regiment.

This photo of the front right end of M1A2 number three of the 2nd Platoon, Dragon Troop, 3rd Armored Cavalry Regiment, was taken five minutes after the preceding photo. The right compensating idler has been pushed far above its normal operating range.

Almost an hour after the preceding photo was shot, one of the M88A2s is parked next to the disabled M1A2. Part of the damaged right track of the tank has been pulled forward and is lying folded on the pavement. The front right fender is still in the raised position.

Work is being done to the right-side running gear of an Abrams. The outer compensating idler wheel has been removed and is standing upright on the ground, and the soldier to the right is working on the inner compensating idler wheel.

At al-Mahmûdîyah, Iraq, in July 2005, a power pack is being lifted from an M1A1 of Troop E, 108th Cavalry Regiment. A crew can remove the power pack, comprising the turbine engine, transmission, oil coolers, and related systems, in about 20 minutes.

A destroyed M1A2 has been loaded onto a M1000 heavy equipment transporter semi-trailer. The catastrophic damage to the tank includes a collapsed suspension, probably a result of the torsion bars failing in the intense heat of a fire in the interior of the tank.

The same destroyed M1A2 is viewed from the left rear of the hull. A tow bar is still in the clamp-type stowage brackets on the side of the hull. Protruding above the roof of the turret is the commander's .50-caliber machine gun mount; the gun is missing.

On the same date the preceding two photos were taken, 1 September 2005, the destroyed M1A2 is being hoisted by two M88A2 Hercules armored recovery vehicles. The left track is hanging loosely, but the right suspension and track were fused in place.

The same destroyed M1A2 now rests on the ground at a base camp in Iraq. The fire that ravaged the vehicle had different effects on the metal and paint of the tank, as is evident in the range of colorations of the side skirts, hull plates, turret, and accessories.

This view of the destroyed M1A2 was taken from near the front right of the hull facing to the rear. To the rear of the A on the side skirt is the open door of the pioneer tool box, which is recessed in the top of the hull. The CITV is visible atop the turret.

This final view of the destroyed M1A2 faces the rear of the hull, with the turret traversed to the rear. Traces of the L-shaped Velcro strips that held the combat identification panels to the front of the turret are still in evidence. This hulk no doubt was beyond repair.

Two M1A2s of the 2nd Platoon, Crazyhorse Troop, 1st Squadron, 3rd Armored Cavalry Regiment, are in position between two Bradleys of the same troop. The rear M1A2 has one black ring around the bore evacuator, indicating it is the platoon leader's tank.

Mechanics are gathered around an Abrams MBT of Dragon Troop, 3rd Armored Cavalry, while a repair or maintenance operation is being performed on the front of the right suspension. The hinged side-skirt panels provide ready access to the suspension.

A sand devil twists away in the background in this view of M1A2s and other vehicles at a base camp in Iraq. The second Abrams from the left has what appears to be a crossed-sabers insignia on the turret, indicating an armored cavalry unit. Visible in the background are several HEMTT M978 10-ton fuel trucks and M977 HEMTT cargo trucks; and, to the left, what appears to be an M109A6 Paladin self-propelled howitzer.

An M1A2 that was severely damaged by a mine blast is being prepared for hoisting onto a semi-trailer for transport to another area. Most of the bogie wheels and side skirts are absent, apparently blown off by the blast, and two remaining skirts are twisted around.

The other side of the mine-damaged M1A2 looks little better. Some bogie wheels are missing, and several side skirts are barely hanging on. Other skirt sections that had been blown off of the tank are piled up on the forward deck to the front of the turret.

Two M88A2 Hercules armored recovery vehicles, their spades dug into the ground to brace the front ends of their suspensions against the strain of lifting the tank, have begun to hoist the damaged M1A2. The tank's tracks have just begun to clear the ground.

The M1A2 has fully cleared the ground and is hanging suspended between the two M88A2s. Visible in the background below the tracks of the M1A2 is the M1000 heavy equipment transporter semi-trailer that will carry the tank to a different location.

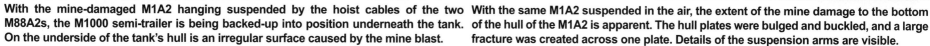

With the mine-damaged M1A2 hanging suspended by the hoist cables of the two M88A2s, the M1000 semi-trailer is being backed-up into position underneath the tank. On the underside of the tank's hull is an irregular surface caused by the mine blast.

Now relocated, the mine-damaged M1A2 sits by a Quonset hut. Among other damage, the fender is crumpled. Indicative of the severity of the blast is the fact that the top hinge of the forward skirt panel is sheared off and its remnants dangle from the fender.

With the same M1A2 suspended in the air, the extent of the mine damage to the bottom of the hull of the M1A2 is apparent. The hull plates were bulged and buckled, and a large fracture was created across one plate. Details of the suspension arms are visible.

The same M1A2 is viewed from the front right. It was being cannibalized for spare parts, since several skirt panels and the coaxial machine gun flash suppressor, which were present when the vehicle was being prepared for transport, are now missing.

A USMC M1A1 provides security while Marines search a village for insurgents in Iraq on 14 November 2005. Dust covers are present on the muzzles of the 120mm main gun and the coaxial machine gun. Green plastic sand bags are arranged on the turret roof.

At Morehead City, North Carolina, in November 2005, an M1A1 of the 22nd Marine Expeditionary Unit is being loaded onto a U.S. Navy landing craft, air cushion. Although the tank is painted overall in green, the combat identification panels are sand colored.

Another M1A1 is being loaded onto LCAC-36 at Morehead City in November 2005, preparatory to shipment to Iraq on the dock landing ship USS *Carter Hall* (LSD-50). The bright-metal tube on top of the turret is one of the towers of the deep-water fording kit.

While many Abrams and crews were committed to the Persian Gulf, elsewhere around the globe crews trained with their vehicles for possible conflict. Here, crewmen of U.S. Army M1A1 Abrams MBTs make preparations for a live-fire exercise at the Rodriguez Live Fire Complex, Republic of Korea, on 19 March 2005. Troops assigned to the 1st Squadron, 1st Calvary Regiment, and 1st Battalion, 72nd Armored Regiment, participated in the exercise. The considerable hot air radiating from the turbine powerplants is distorting the background in this photo.

An M1A2 Abrams tank crew of 2nd Platoon, Bandit Troop, 1st Squadron, 3rd Armored Cavalry Regiment prepares for a mission at Forward Operating Base Heider in Rabî'ah, Iraq, on 27 June 2005. Abundant details are visible on the top of the vehicle.

Clad in interceptor body armor and Kevlar helmets, five soldiers – one more than the number in an Abrams crew – relax on the turret. The unit markings on the front of the hull indicate this is an Abrams MBT of the 3rd Squadron, 3rd Armored Cavalry Regiment.

Sergeant First Class John Guy of the 2nd Battalion, 3rd Armored Cavalry Regiment, is at the commander's weapon station of his M1A2 during a patrol in Tal'afar, Iraq, on 19 January 2006. A good view is provided of the M2 HB .50-caliber machine gun.

Crewmen of an Abrams MBT are on high alert as they conduct a combat patrol in Tal'afar, Iraq, on 2 February 2006. A tow bar suspended on clevises is available should a rapid recovery be required. Scrawled on the front plate of the hull is "G43."

Crews of two **M1A2 Abrams MBTs** of the 3rd Armored Cavalry Regiment conduct a combat patrol in the city of Tal'afar, Iraq, on 3 February 2005. Combat identification panels are not present on the turrets; the nearer tank has a ballistic shield with windows on the loader's machine gun mount. Dark-colored paint has been applied to areas of the front panels of the turret, evidently to cover earlier markings.

Two M1A1s, including one in the foreground with fittings for mine-clearance blades, occupy a position in an Iraqi town. The side skirts and lower parts of the turrets are coated with mud. Stenciled on the gun barrel of the closer tank is "Amber Lynne."

Markings on the front of the hull of this M1A2 are for K Troop, 3rd Squadron, 3rd Armored Cavalry Regiment. The lengthy combination of numbers and letters at the upper center of the front hull plate is the vehicle's Department of Defense shipping number.

Private First Class Joseph Grace of the 1st Armored Division relaxes by throwing a football in front of an Abrams MBT before the beginning of a patrol mission in Tal'afar, Iraq, in February 2006. The commander's .50-caliber machine gun is fitted with a cover.

During nighttime, the power pack of a U.S. Marine Corps Abrams main battle tank is suspended above the tank. The Abrams tank's AGT-1500 gas turbine engine produce twice the gross horsepower of the engine of the Abrams' predecessor, the M60A1, resulting in much improved speed and acceleration. The engine consumes vast quantities of air, and after the First Gulf War, the problems with constantly having to clean air filters in dusty environments was solved when a pulse-jet air-filter-cleaning system was developed for the M1A1 and M1A2.

A U.S. Army M1A1 Abrams MBT conducts a patrol mission near Tal'afar, Iraq, on 17 May 2006. The number 30 is painted on a side-skirt panel and on a panel at the rear of the turret bustle. Two rolls of concertina wire are carried at the rear of the hull. These are held in place by a several steel channel-type posts secured together and stuck through the lifting eyes at the rear of the hull

Crewmen of an M1A2 of Alpha Company, 1st Battalion, 66th Armored Regiment provide security for Shî'ah on their annual pilgrimage to Karbalâ', Iraq. The number 432 is painted in black on the front side-skirt panel. The fenders and 120mm barrel are green.

A marine mechanic performs repairs on an M1A1 at Camp Al-Fallûjah, Iraq, on 21 January 2007. The Abrams was assigned to Regimental Combat Team 6. Two of the side-skirt panels are swung open, allowing easy access to the suspension components.

During combined-arms training at the Novo Selo Training Area in Bulgaria, U.S. Army personnel and Bulgarian soldiers inspect and compare notes on, left to right, two T-72 Main Battle Tanks, an Abrams MBT, and a Bradley Fighting Vehicle.

The crew of an Abrams MBT of the 3rd Battalion, 69th Armor Regiment, searches for possible weapons caches at Buhayrat ath-Tharthâr (Lake Tharthâr), north of Baghdâd, during joint Coalition-Iraqi Operation Fawat Al Asad on 17 November 2007.

Marine crewmen of an M1A1 prepare for a mission at Camp Al-Fallûjah, Iraq, on 21 January 2007. The loader's machine gun was omitted on some Marine Abrams, such as this one, to improve the commander's visibility while operating in urban areas.

Tank crewmen and other personnel of Task Force 1-77, 1st Battalion, 18th Infantry Regiment, 3rd Infantry Division, finalize preparations for staging a convoy out of Camp Ramâdî, Iraq, on 4 October 2007. Two M1A1s and an M88 recovery vehicle are in view.

At Combat Outpost Râwah, Iraq, on 26 April 2007, Lt. Sean Olone, an electronic warfare officer, briefs Capt. Garry Mace, USN, on the Counter Radio-controlled improvised explosive device Electronic Warfare (CREW) equipment on an M1A1. The CREW is designed to defeat improvised explosive devices (IEDs) that are detonated by radio signal.

A U.S. Army M1A1 conducts an anti-IED operation on a highway in Baghdâd on 22 December 2007. This tank is equipped with a recently updated tank urban survivability (TUSK) kit to better enable it to withstand attacks by insurgents. This kit includes a low armored shield on the turret roof around the loader's hatch, reactive armor tiles that replaced the hull skirts, a thermal sight and searchlight for the tank commander's .50 caliber machine gun, an additional .50 caliber machine gun mounted over the main gun, and a thermal sight for the loader's M240MG.

An M1A2 demonstrates a TUSK suite in Iraq in April 2008. The key feature seen here is the array of reactive-armor tiles applied to the side skirts, to better defeat enemy-fired projectiles in this vulnerable area. Other enhancements are also available in TUSK.

A U.S. Army M1A1 upgraded with TUSK was photographed in Baghdâd on 22 December 2007. Features include extra armor plating for the loader's machine gun station, spotlights, and a mount for a .50-caliber machine gun above the mantlet.

These two TUSK-equipped M1A1s of D Company 2nd Battalion, 69th Armor, 3rd BCT, 3ID, are readying for a patrol in Iraq on 7 December 2007. Extra .50-caliber machine guns are installed on their mounts by the ammunition boxes above the 120mm gun mantlet.

This is a loader's-eye view of M1A1s with TUSK conducting a counter-IED mission in Baghdâd in December 2007. In the foreground are a mount for an extra .50-caliber machine gun (not mounted), its ammunition box, and several spotlights.

This M1A2 with TUSK has shields fitted not only to the loader's machine gun mount but also the commander's. The .50-caliber machine gun mounted over the mantlet was synched to elevate with the 120mm gun, acting as an additional coaxial machine gun.

Two soldiers are adjusting the .50-caliber M2 HB machine gun of the commander's weapon station on an Abrams. This CWS has received a ballistic shield with windows partially surrounding it and a ballistic shield, also with windows, on the gun mount.

The angled fillet at the front edge of the reactive armor tiles of TUSK is visible. The front and sides of the hull and the turret receive no armor enhancements under TUSK since these areas are already deemed sufficiently strong to defeat enemy projectiles.

TUSK armor is displayed on an M1A2 roof, including the ballistic shield partially surrounding the CWS, the shield on the commander's machine gun mount, the two-piece shield on the loader's gun mount, and fixed armor around the loader's hatch.

This M1A2 turret lacks TUSK improvements. The commander's hatch cover opens to several different configurations, including one to protect the commander's back, seen here, and one to give him overhead protection while looking out of the hatch.

The same M1A2 with TUSK in the preceding photo exits through a gate, displaying to better effect the rear of its hull. The extra coaxial .50-caliber machine gun is not installed in its mount above the mantlet. Two vertical steel channels are on the rear grilles.

Turret pointed to the rear, an M1A2 with TUSK gets underway at a base camp in Iraq. Some Abrams tanks with TUSK have bar armor installed on the rear of the hull to protect that vulnerable area from projectiles, but this M1A2 lacks that armor installation.

A U.S. Marine Corps Abrams of Alpha Company, 4th Tank Battalion, proceeds through the al-Jazîrah Desert in western Iraq's al-Anbâr Province on 20 June 2008. On the left side of the turret is what appears to be an anti-IED antenna.

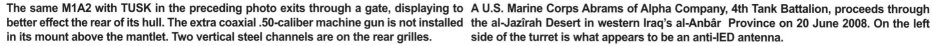

On 5 January 2008, Landing Craft, Air Cushion 8 (LCAC-8) offloads an M1A1 Abrams tank of the 11th Marine Expeditionary Unit in Kuwait, where the unit was conducting training exercises. This vehicle has the external EAPU at the top left of the turret bustle.

Gunnery Sgt. Samuel T. Swain of the 2nd Battalion, 5th Marine Regiment, stands behind the .50-caliber machine gun in the commander's weapon station of his M1A1 during exercises at the National Training Center in Fort Irwin, California, in March 2008.

An M1A2 with TUSK enhancements moves through a base camp during nighttime. Visible are the reactive armor tiles on the side skirts, the ballistic shield for the loader's machine gun, and the mount and ammunition box for the extra coaxial machine gun.

The M1A2 with TUSK is viewed from more to the rear. Above the roof of the turret, the low armor plate next to the outboard side of the loader's hatch, added as part of the TUSK enhancements, is visible. The tapered rear fillet of the reactive armor is in view.

In the background of this scene of an M88A2 being used to unload supplies is a marine Abrams MBT of Company A, 4th Tank Battalion, Task Force Mech (TF Mech), Multi-National Force-West. Two CREW antennas are mounted on the side of the turret.

Two USMC M1A1s of the 1st Tank Battalion, I Marine Expeditionary force, are parked next to a shelter at Combat Outpost Mudaysis, Iraq, on 3 October 2008. A shelter was rigged over the turret of the tank to the left to give the crew relief from the hot sun.

The crews of M1A1 registration number 633188 of the 2nd Tank Battalion and an amphibious assault vehicle from the 2nd Assault Amphibian Battalion undergo training at Marine Corps Air Ground Combat Center, Twentynine Palms, California, in 2009.

A column of M1A1s of C Company, 1st Tank Battalion, proceed through Noble Pass at the Marine Corps Air Ground Combat Center, Twentynine Palms, California, on 14 April 2009. The lead vehicle has a downward-pointing chevron on the front side skirt.

Marine M1A1, registration number 633186, provides covering fire for infantrymen during training exercises at Twentynine Palms in June 2009. The marking 2-3 is stenciled on the fenders, and a scorpion insignia is painted in black on the smoke-grenade box.

On the well deck of the amphibious dock landing ship USS *Fort McHenry* (LSD-43) in the Mediterranean in October 2009, Marines of the 22nd Marine Expeditionary Unit employ an M88A2 Hercules recovery vehicle to replace the engine of an M1A1 Abrams.

Teamwork is on display as Marines of Combat Logistics Battalion 22 of the 22nd Marine Expeditionary Unit work to replace the engine of an M1A1 Abrams MBT resting on a tarp on the well deck of USS *Fort McHenry* (LSD-43) on 15 October 2009. Toward the bottom of the photo is the forward end of the gas turbine engine. "NO STEP" is marked prominently at several places on the bare-metal exhaust duct.

Four M1A2 Abrams MBTs with TUSK and CREW enhancements are parked at a base. All four tanks have ballistic shields around the commander's cupola, a shield on the commander's machine gun mount, and the mount for an extra coaxial machine gun. (Russ Adams)

M1A1s of the Tank platoon, 24th Marine Expeditionary Unit, undergo joint exercises with French counterparts at a live-firing range in Djibouti on the Horn of Africa on 30 March 2010. At the rear of the hull is the elbow fitting for the deep-water fording kit.

In a photo taken from atop the roof of the turret of a marine M1A1 conducting live-firing exercises in Djibouti on 30 March 2010, Lance Cpl. William Laffoon of Tank Platoon, Alpha Company, 24th Marine Expeditionary Unit, is in the loader's hatch as the tank's 120mm main gun fires. Marine M1A1s engaged several targets in cooperation with the French 13th Foreign Legion Demi-Brigade. Close-up views are offered of the loader's 7.62mm M240 machine gun on a skate-ring mount and part of the commander's .50-caliber machine gun mount.

An M1A1 Abrams MBT is outfitted with a mine-clearing blade (MCB), sometimes referred to as a Track Width Mine Plow (TWMP). The unit, operated by an electric motor, weighs around 6,940 pounds can be installed on an Abrams in about one hour. The outer sides of the MCB comprise blade assemblies; the lower part of each assembly has teeth to extract mines, a moldboard (seen folded down here) to push mines to the side, and leveling skids inboard of the blades to regulate the depth of the blade. The MCB creates two cleared paths, each of which is almost five feet wide. A "dog bone" suspended between the blades detonates tilt-rod mines and magnetic mines.

An Abrams MBT with CREW and TUSK enhancements is loaded on an M1000 heavy equipment transporter semi-trailer coupled to an Oshkosh M1070 truck tractor. Together, the M1070 and M1000 comprise the Heavy Equipment Transport System (HETS). (Russ Adams)

A soldier motions the driver of an Abrams MBT into place on an M1000 heavy equipment transporter semi-trailer. This particular tank has TUSK and CREW enhancements. Stenciled in black on the bore evacuator of the 120mm main gun is *Duck Hunt*. (Russ Adams)

This M1A1 positioned on an M1000 semi-trailer coupled to an Oshkosh M1070 truck tractor is being prepared for off-loading. A track chock is lying on the ground next to the semi-trailer. To the right are another M1000 semi-trailer and a potable water tanker. (Russ Adams)

The same M1A1 shown in the preceding photo is being backed off the M1000 semi-trailer. A CREW antenna is atop the turret bustle. To the left, a vehicle has just been unloaded from the other M1000, and the ramps have been raised to their stowed position. (Russ Adams)

Mechanics have removed the powerpack from this M1A1, providing a view into the engine compartment. Two access hatches are open to the front left of the compartment, and the cooler and exhaust grilles at the rear of the compartment are swung open. The engine compartment is painted white. On the rear of the right side of the compartment is the right final-drive housing. This M1A1 also exhibits details of the TUSK and CREW enhancements. (Russ Adams)

In another view of the same M1A1 shown in the preceding photo, a mechanic makes adjustments in the engine compartment. The rough, non-skid surface on the access doors is visible. Details of the TUSK armor and enhancements are also revealed.

Several Abrams powerpacks lie in a vehicular maintenance yard. Keeping the engines in proper operating condition is essential to the success of the Abrams in combat. In the background are a crane for hoisting the powerpacks and an M1A1 Abrams MBT.

An M1A2 of the 3rd Armored Cavalry Regiment on the firing range at Forward Operating Base Hammer, Wâsiṭ, Iraq, in 2011 has a Muzzle Boresight Device (MBD) inserted in the bore of the 120mm gun for checking that the bore of the gun is aligned with the sights.

A loadmaster signals the driver of an Abrams MBT boarding a C-5M Super Galaxy of the 436th Airlift Wing, at Dover Air Force Base, Delaware, in November 2011, as part of an attempt by the wing to score several new world records on that day.

Two M1A1s assigned to Delta Company, 1st Tank Battalion, 1st Marine Division, are parked at Forward Operating Base Edinburgh in Helmand Province, Afghanistan, on 2 February 2011. This unit was supporting the International Security Assistance Force. On the tank to the left, a tow bar is attached to the front end, and the fenders are raised. The M1A1 to the right is fitted with a Pearson Blade, Direct Fit, M1 dozer blade.

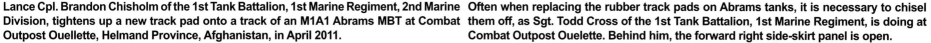

In another photo taken at Forward Operating Base Edinburgh on 2 February 2011, a Delta Company, 1st Tank Battalion, M1A1 is being fueled. The Abrams MBT in the background is fitted with a mine-clearing blade; both tanks have CREW antennas.

A very clean USMC M1A1, serial number 632668, is staged behind the insignia of the 2nd Marine Division on the parade deck at Camp Leatherneck, Helmand Province, Afghanistan, during a transfer-of-authority ceremony on 15 March 2011.

Lance Cpl. Brandon Chisholm of the 1st Tank Battalion, 1st Marine Regiment, 2nd Marine Division, tightens up a new track pad onto a track of an M1A1 Abrams MBT at Combat Outpost Ouellette, Helmand Province, Afghanistan, in April 2011.

Often when replacing the rubber track pads on Abrams tanks, it is necessary to chisel them off, as Sgt. Todd Cross of the 1st Tank Battalion, 1st Marine Regiment, is doing at Combat Outpost Ouelette. Behind him, the forward right side-skirt panel is open.

Members of the 3rd Armored Cavalry Regiment undergo tank qualifications with an M1A2 Abrams MBT at Forward Operating Base Hammer, in Wâsiṭ, Iraq, in 2011. TUSK enhancements include reactive-armor tiles, shields, and extra coaxial machine gun mount.

Australia is among the countries that have acquired the Abrams MBT. The crew commander and loader of this Australian M1A1 are with the 1st Armoured Regiment. Close-up views also are provided of the "dog house" over the gunner's primary sight and the machine guns.

Kuwait is an operator of the Abrams Main Battle tank, including these M1A2s participating in a parade at Camp 'Arifjân, Kuwait, in 2011. Green combat identification panels on the fronts and sides of the turrets contrast with the sand color of the tanks.

In 2011, Iraq purchased 140 Abrams tanks, including these M1A1s parked at a secured compound at the Bismâyah Combat Training Center, through a foreign military sales agreement with the United States. The last shipment arrived in August 2011.

Iraqi M1A1 crewmen of the 9th Mechanized Division are learning to drive the M1A1 in a column of march during the M1A1 Operators of New Equipment Training Course at the Bismâyah Combat Training Center, Baghdâd, in March 2011. All turrets are trained to the rear.

A USMC M1A1 with TUSK armor guards a bridge crossing near Combat Outpost Ouellette in Helmand province, Afghanistan, in April 2011. This Abrams tank was assigned to the 1st Platoon, Delta Company, 1st Marine Tank Battalion.

Crewmen of M1A1 Abrams MBTs of Alpha Company, 2nd Marine Tank Battalion, make preparations to refuel their tanks at Combat Outpost Shir Ghazay, Afghanistan. The first tank has a tow bar attached to the front end for speedy recovery if necessary.

M1A1s of Alpha Company, 2nd Tank Battalion, 2nd Marine Division, stand down at Combat Outpost Shir Ghazay, Helmand Province, Afghanistan, after a 24-hour overwatch mission, during which they provided security for Coalition forces.

Two M1A1s of Alpha Company, 2nd Marine Tank Battalion, including one in the foreground and registration number 632668 in the background, are employed in an overwatch mission at Combat Outpost Shir Ghazay, Afghanistan.

M1A1 crewmen of Alpha Company, 2nd Tank Battalion, 2nd Marine Division, work through the night at Combat Outpost Shir Ghazay to complete maintenance on their tank. For every hour of operation, the M1A1 required up to ten hours of maintenance.

At Combat Outpost Shir Ghazay, Afghanistan, Marines of Alpha Company, 2nd Tank Battalion, 2nd Marine Division (Forward), emerge from an M1A1 after completing a 24-hour overwatch mission. Even when fighting was not involved, this type of duty was arduous, particularly during the daylight hours, when it was necessary to sit in the tank for hours on end in the hot sun.

79

Marines of 1st Platoon, Alpha Company, 2nd Tank Battalion, are silhouetted by the low sun on their M1A1 Abrams along the Iraqi-Syrian border during Operation Iraqi Freedom. For over three decades, the M1 Abrams series of main battle tanks and their crews and support personnel have given stellar service, proving themselves time and again on the front lines of the cold war and in several hot wars in the Persian Gulf and Central Asia. The Abrams is slated to remain in service for many more years, and with proper modernizations, the tank will soldier on for years to come.